Original title:
The House Beyond the Horizon

Copyright © 2025 Creative Arts Management OÜ
All rights reserved.

Author: Evan Hawthorne
ISBN HARDBACK: 978-1-80587-177-4
ISBN PAPERBACK: 978-1-80587-647-2

## Nature's Whimsy on the Other Side

In the garden where gnomes giggle,
Rabbits wear socks and wiggle.
Butterflies painted bright and bold,
Tell secrets that never get old.

Trees dance to songs of the breeze,
Swaying in rhythm with utmost ease.
Squirrels throw acorns like balls,
While mushrooms answer with funny calls.

## Alluring Hues of the Great Beyond

Pinks and purples mix for fun,
Under skies where odd clouds run.
A rainbow's laugh is a silly tune,
Sung by a very giggly moon.

Lollipop hills with candy streams,
Where candy canes fulfill your dreams.
Fish in polka dots swim with flair,
Winking and nodding without a care.

## Migrations of the Ungrateful Heart

A bird packed bags but lost its map,
Thought it could fly but fell in a lap.
Turned around, it eats a seed,
Now more concerned with its next feed.

Lovebirds argue over the best snack,
One says worms, the other, a quack.
With hearts so big but manners so poor,
They leave witty notes at each other's door.

## Tranquility Beyond the Setting Sun

Sunsets giggle in shades of chai,
As cats roll by, oh my, oh my!
Pigs in pajamas waddle on through,
Laughing and cheering, 'How do you do?'

Stars play hopscotch, twinkling with glee,
While crickets gather for tea at three.
Moonbeams shimmer with a chuckle slight,
Whispering dreams tucked in the night.

## Whispers of Distant Abodes

In a place where socks all roam,
The garden gnomes have found a home.
They gossip in the light of day,
And steal your snacks in sneaky play.

Kites are tied to fussy cats,
They've formed a union with the bats.
The clouds above are made of cheese,
And time is spent on silly pleas.

Chickens dance with flair and grace,
While rabbits race in a comical chase.
The moon is just a big round pie,
And stars jump high, oh my, oh my!

So if you peek into the trees,
You'll find a place of fun and knees.
A laughter-filled abode for all,
With silly pranks and one big ball.

## Shadows on the Twilight Ridge

In shadows cast by twilight's wink,
The paper airplanes start to think.
They plot a flight to lands of fun,
While teddy bears bask in the sun.

The squirrels wear hats of bright design,
As acorns roll like small divine.
The evening breeze hums a soft tune,
And disco balls twirl with the moon.

Llamas gossip in the fields,
About the love that sunshine yields.
Each blade of grass knows all the jokes,
And even quiet trees will poke.

Runnin' down the twilight lane,
With giggles echoing in the rain.
So join the dance till morning breaks,
As sunshine spills like sweet pancakes.

## Dreams Sheltered in Dusk

Underneath the twilight's cloak,
The rubber ducks begin to soak.
They float around with joyful glee,
In puddles made for you and me.

A team of squirrels plays charades,
While fireflies light up the glades.
A cat in shades surveys the scene,
With paws that tap the beat so keen.

The dreams of socks get knotted tight,
In playful spins they take their flight.
And giggles spill from leafy bows,
As pixies form their secret vows.

So linger in that dusky spell,
Where wishes come and laughter dwells.
In puffs of night the stories bloom,
And chase away all sense of gloom.

## Echoes of the Unseen Refuge

Invisible walls hold tales untold,
Where pirates wear the silliest gold.
They ride on clouds and laugh out loud,
While elephants dance in the crowd.

In hidden nooks, the dreams take flight,
With unicorns in starry night.
The daisies chat with butterflies,
And secrets hide behind their sighs.

Around the bend, a jester plays,
With juggling stars and funny ways.
The fish can swim through clouds of foam,
In this abode where quirks feel home.

So wander soft through laughter's door,
To echoes of silliness and more.
For in this spot, you'll laugh and cheer,
As joy unfolds and shadows disappear.

## **Cradled by the Distant Horizon**

In a place where socks go rogue,
And laundry finds a way to bogue,
A cat in a hat sings a tune,
While dancing with a giant balloon.

The sun wears shades with style and grace,
A bicycle holds a happy face,
The trees tell jokes that tickle your ear,
As laughter echoes far and near.

## Beyond the Lines of Time

A clock that runs on jellybeans,
Counts every joke and silly scenes,
While wizards brew a fizzy drink,
And mimes make us laugh without a wink.

The teacups chat with tiny glee,
Beneath a sky as bright as a bee,
Each second plays a prancing part,
Tickling both mind and heart.

## The Enchantment of Faraway Dreams

In dreams where penguins wear neat ties,
And everyone speaks in goofy sighs,
A marshmallow elephant takes a ride,
On a rainbow slide with a jellyfish guide.

Stars giggle as they dance in pairs,
While cupcakes twirl in glittery airs,
Life's a circus, hilariously grand,
With each odd twist, a comedic hand.

## **Nestled in the Silent Whisper**

Whispers travel on fluffy clouds,
Singing secrets to curious crowds,
Where the shadows play leapfrog down,
And wear invisible capes of brown.

A squirrel plays chess with a wise old cat,
Discussing the best way to lose a hat,
While snickering trees help pass the time,
In this place where laughter is sublime.

## The Allure of Unknown Waters

A boat was built with a squeaky wheel,
It danced on waves, what a comical deal!
Fish wore hats, sipping tea so grand,
While crabs played cards on the soft, golden sand.

The sun wore glasses, not to get burned,
While dolphins laughed for the world they turned.
They splashed around, making quite a mess,
As seagulls joined in, looking chic in their dress.

Mermaids juggling pearls, what a sight!
Singing so loudly into the night.
The octopus played chess with a seal,
In this quirky world, everything's surreal!

So if you wander, take a look near,
At waters unknown, and pack some cheer.
For laughter bubbles where the waves twirl,
In a wacky world, let your dreams unfurl.

## Cradled by Distant Shores

On distant sands, a camel wore shoes,
Prancing in circles, amusing the blues.
Seagulls competed in a dance-off so bright,
While turtles cheered under the warm, yellow light.

Palm trees tilted, trying to peek,
At a hermit crab's highly-skilled streak.
With each little shuffle, it drew quite a crowd,
As laughter erupted, and silliness loud.

The ocean waved, 'Come and join in,'
While starfish debated if they could spin.
And if you asked the sand, it giggled and shrugged,
In this wacky realm, no one was mugged!

So gather your chums, make some sandy art,
In a land where the laughter just won't depart.
For here every moment's a chance to rejoice,
In a delightful place where the waves have a voice.

# Unveiling the Hidden Realm

In a realm where shadows play hide-and-seek,
A raccoon wore socks and let out a squeak.
Trees wore spectacles, reading green books,
While frogs sat in chairs, giving curious looks.

A rabbit proclaimed, 'I'm the ruler of fate!'
Turning his nose at the pastries on plate.
In twilight's glow, the oddities meet,
With whispers of giggles in this cheeky retreat.

Clouds donned hats, swirling with glee,
As the moon took selfies, 'Look at me!'
Where unicorns napped on marshmallow beds,
And laughter kept floating around in their heads.

So venture forth into this silly parade,
Where laughter erupts and memories are made.
For in this bright land of whimsical sights,
Even the stars twinkle with giggles at nights.

## Portals to the Unknown Realm

A door creaks loud, like a rusty hinge,
A cat jumps high, it's seen a fringe.
The room is odd, with socks in pairs,
These portals grant a world of wares.

A fridge that hums an ancient song,
Where leftovers dance and twirl along.
Time bends here, it's quite a ride,
A piece of cheese might serve as guide.

So jump right in, let chaos reign,
In this realm where logic's slain.
A carpet flies, you grab a snack,
Unplug the clock, there's no turning back.

In the end, a laugh or two,
With cosmic jokes no one knew.
So venture far, embrace the thrill,
For in this space, it's fun to chill.

## The Sanctuary at Day's End

The sun sinks low, the shadows creep,
The old dog snores, he's lost in sleep.
A garden gnome winks, he's up to no good,
Plotting a prank near the tall wood.

Here lies a chair that squeaks with glee,
Always ready for company.
A squirrel in a top hat brings the tea,
In this haven, we all feel free.

The lawnmower sings a sweet refrain,
While neighbors argue who's to blame.
But over the fence, a pie does fly,
With giggles echoing in the sky.

So gather round as stars appear,
In this silly place, there's naught to fear.
For laughter fills the evening air,
As friendships bloom everywhere.

## Lighthouses in the Ethereal Mist

A lighthouse beams, and oh, what fun,
Guiding lost ships 'til day is done.
But wait, what's that? A fish in a hat?
Is that normal? It surely is not that!

The fog rolls in with a whimsical twist,
Where seagulls squawk and waves insist.
A boat sails by with a strange old man,
Who offers up soup from a rusty can.

Tall tales float like the misty spray,
Of mermaids gossiping at the bay.
While monsters play charades on the shore,
It's a wacky night—who could ask for more?

So raise a glass to the quirky crew,
In this lighthouse land, where dreams come true.
For laughter echoes through the beams,
In a place that's woven from whimsical dreams.

## **Footsteps on the Silent Trail**

The trail is quiet, but not for long,
With whispers and giggles, it feels like a song.
A squirrel sizes up a passing shoe,
"Hey, who's there? I want some stew!"

Each step we take on this winding path,
Brings us closer to a friendly laugh.
A tree that dances, oh, what a sight,
With leaves that shimmer like fairy light.

What's that? A bench that seems to grin,
As if inviting all the folk in.
Sharing stories of both tall and small,
In this hush, there's room for all.

So let's keep walking, let's skip and hop,
In a world where silly never stops.
For footsteps here lead to joy and cheer,
In a secret space where friends draw near.

## Under the Canopy of Possibility

In a land where dreams wear hats,
Socks dance along with chatting cats.
Unicorns try to sell you shoes,
While jellybeans sing the morning blues.

Rainbows weave through lemonade streams,
And goofy fish swim in crazy dreams.
A giant snail claims to be a chef,
Serving up sandwiches, a bit of a mess.

Lollipops grow on trees with flair,
While squirrels argue in midair.
At sunrise, the pancakes take flight,
And tuck the sleepy sun in tight.

So come on down and bring your cheer,
To this place where laughter's near.
Life's a giggle, a goofy thrill,
In the land of wonky goodwill.

## The Refuge of Faraway Echoes

Whispers float on the warm breeze,
Telling tales of cheese and peas.
A rabbit wears spectacles, quite absurd,
Reciting poetry to an ill-mannered bird.

The clock strikes seven with a little doubt,
As toasters toast toast with a shout.
Dancing with muffins in fluffy shoes,
While jellybeans swap their colored hues.

Faraway echoes chuckle and play,
Making silly sounds that bounce away.
A parrot critiques a cat's ballet,
While dreaming of fish for dinner today.

So wander here, with your humor intact,
To a place where giggles never lack.
In this refuge of laughter's delight,
Every echo sings through the night.

## Lanterns Guiding Lost Souls

Balloons float past on a windy trail,
Guiding lost souls with a giggle and wail.
A dancing light with a winking grin,
Leads the way to adventure within.

In this land of lanterns and bright dreams,
Picnic ants host fancy ice cream themes.
Bacon-flavored clouds drift in the sky,
Where candy corn rain brings a sugary high.

Silly shadows trip on their way,
Creating laughter at the end of the day.
Wishes ride on the back of a kite,
With a flurry of fun till it's quite night.

So follow the glow, don't be shy,
Where the giggles bounce high and dreams fly.
Each lantern a chuckle, a joyful goal,
In this whimsical dance of jesting souls.

## **Unraveled Threads of Distant Places**

From a spool of laughter, ribbons unwind,
Weaving tales of the silly kind.
Mice in top hats play chess with flair,
While turtles race on a squeaky chair.

In corners of dreams where giggles collide,
A camel juggles with undeniable pride.
Wizards with wands made of whimsical fluff,
Charm the clouds, but it's never enough.

Oh, the buttons on shirts that cackle and squeak,
Turning serious moments into a cheeky peak.
Cupcakes throw parties at midnight's ring,
As a flurry of sprinkles take off on a swing.

So wander through where the laughter treads,
Unraveled threads and nonsense spreads.
In this colorful tapestry of fun,
Each stitch a chuckle, forever spun.

## Haunting Melodies of Yesterday

In a realm where echoes play,
Ghosts of snacks from yesterday.
They dance in kitchens, swirl like mist,
But still can't find a pot to whisk.

Socks are lost, they join the fun,
Hiding from chores, they start to run.
A broomstick's got a mind of its own,
Sweeping secrets, but never shone.

The fridge hums a silly tune,
As leftovers plot by the light of the moon.
Spiders spin their webs with flair,
Adventures dance on dusty air.

Old hats gossip, spinning their tales,
Of mischief, laughter, and snail mail trails.
They say the past's not truly dead,
Especially when you trip on bread.

## The Unfolding of Hidden Corners

Under beds where dust bunnies lay,
A treasure map to yesterday.
Call your socks, they'll make a fuss,
As they try to board the old school bus.

In every cupboard, tales unfold,
Of rogue tupperwares and whimsy bold.
Lost toys whisper secrets of cheer,
They've never left; they just disappeared.

The cat's in charge, or so it seems,
Plotting world takeovers in her dreams.
She leads the charge with a flick of her tail,
While yarn balls become the holy grail.

A chair creaks low, it's got a joke,
Of missed appointments and coffee smoke.
Every shadow's a friend in disguise,
As laughter dances under twilight skies.

## The Legacy of Boundless Living

A garden grows on the kitchen wall,
With herbs that giggle and veggies that thrall.
Thyme insists it's better with cheese,
While spinach just aims to bring you ease.

The clock ticks backward, if you ask,
Time's just a funny little task.
Balloons escape to join the sky,
While cookies whisper, "We've learned to fly!"

Laundry's a circus, oh what a sight,
With shirts that tumble and brights that bite.
A sock parade down the staircase runs,
Performing stunts and hurling puns.

In this chaos, joy takes flight,
With mismatched shoes, they dance all night.
The legacy's laughter, loud and clear,
A home that welcomes every cheer.

## Journeys Through Twinkling Spaces

Stars peek in through the window screen,
In a spaceship made from an old jelly bean.
The couch becomes the captain's chair,
As popcorn heads off into thin air.

We sail through dreams on a river of light,
Chasing shadows till the morning bright.
The frogs in the pond throw a grand parade,
Hopping to songs mistakes have made.

A blanket fort hides a kingdom rare,
With snug pillow dragons and squeaky bears.
Each laugh's a ticket to a place unknown,
Where wild imaginations have fiercely grown.

So grab your snacks, pack up your grin,
Adventure awaits, let the fun begin!
In the depths of the night, joy interlaces,
In journeys we take through twinkling spaces.

## **Nestled Amongst the Clouds**

Up high where the goats wear hats,
A squirrel juggles peanuts with his mats.
Clouds tickle homes like fluffy cakes,
While birds steal pies and dance in lakes.

The sun sips tea on a car parked there,
Chicken suits strut without a care.
The breeze tells jokes that make you snort,
While kites argue in reports of court.

At night the stars play hide and seek,
While moonbeams wear socks and play peek-a-boo geek.
Up here laughter flows like a stream,
As giggles ride on a marshmallow dream.

## **An Odyssey Towards Infinity**

A cat with a map sails on a slice,
Searching for treasure that smells of spice.
The fish in the creek wear googly eyes,
Telling tall tales beneath the skies.

Robots in pajamas dance in line,
While llamas sip cocoa from cups so fine.
Infinite laughter lingers in the air,
As all the trees wear hats with flair.

Somewhere a snail plays chess with a frog,
While ants throw a party on a fallen log.
Time skips like a stone across a pond,
Where wacky creatures form a joyful bond.

## Tales from the Silent Frontier

In a land where silence sings out loud,
Ducks wear tuxedos and dance in a crowd.
Cacti tell stories of cowboys past,
While tumbleweeds giggle and roll by fast.

A whistling wind plays hide-and-seek,
With shadows that wobble and sometimes sneak.
Yonder, a cactus claims to be tall,
But trips on a pebble and starts to sprawl.

Llamas wear capes and fly through the skies,
While tumblebugs plot to make some pies.
In this quiet place, laughter is vast,
As echoes carry the fun, unsurpassed.

## The Lantern That Glows at Dusk

A lantern swings low and throws a grin,
As fireflies quiz each other with a spin.
Ghosts throw a party, they dance with glee,
While pumpkins wear glasses and sip iced tea.

A hedgehog with glasses reads the news,
Telling tales of the cats in fancy shoes.
Under the glow, the raccoons play poker,
With cookies as chips; they're quite the joker.

The owl brings wisdom, but loves to jest,
As woodland creatures join in the fest.
Under the twinkle of stars above,
This dusk-lit gathering is full of love.

## **Echoing Murmurs of Age-Old Myths**

In a realm where the shadows are snickering,
Old tales spring forth, spirits flickering.
A cat in a hat tells a fishy joke,
While the moon's on a pogo, bouncing in smoke.

Through fields of laughter, the nonsense flies,
A dragon that dances with spaghetti ties.
Mermaids in slippers skip on the sand,
With unicorns doing a conga band.

Elves trade their wisdom for pickled fish,
As birds hold court, calling out for a wish.
The trolls under bridges just chuckle and snore,
While giants on stilts play hopscotch galore.

Here myths are a puzzle, each piece a delight,
With giggles and grins illuminating the night.
So come join the party of fanciful lore,
Where laughter is key, and wonders explore.

## Hopes Carried on the Wind

A kite made of dreams sails up to the sky,
With wishes like popcorn, all buttered and high.
The clouds are just pillows where giggles reside,
As raindrops wear hats while they bounce and slide.

Whispers of fairies on bicycles ride,
Through forests of marshmallows, side by side.
Every gust carries chuckles, a jolly parade,
With a rubber chicken leading the cascade.

A squirrel in a tuxedo twirls on a beam,
While frogs in top hats all scramble to dream.
The breeze tells secrets of soda pop streams,
And laughter spills freely, like bubbling ice creams.

So fly your ambitions on winds full of cheer,
Where joy is the currency, gold's worth a tear.
In a land where the sun wears silly-shaped grins,
Find hopes that are carried where laughter begins.

## Serendipity at the Horizon's Edge

At the edge of the day, where silliness sprawls,
A jester juggles jellybeans, giggling in stalls.
The sun wears a bowtie, bright colors in tow,
As the sea sings a tune of a ticklish woe.

Fish in tuxedos play chess with the tides,
While seaweed wiggles, dancing with pride.
Sailboats made of cupcakes float in delight,
Chasing after rainbows that wink in the light.

A crab in a blazer recites goofy rhymes,
As turtles do limbo, defying all times.
Seagulls wear spectacles, squawking profound,
Holding meetings on laughter, discussing joy found.

So join in the frolic, embrace the bizarre,
Where serendipity shines just like a star.
At the horizon's edge, old tales take a spin,
And whimsical moments are where we begin.

## The Illusion of Distant Shores

On a map drawn in crayon, the waves start to dance,
With octopi sporting their finest pants.
Sandcastles guard treasures of laughter and fun,
While starfish hold beauty contests in the sun.

Mermaids sip coffee and play cards with whales,
And jellybeans drift on their wondrous sails.
The sun plays a game of peek-a-boo bright,
As shadows do waltzes, igniting the night.

But wait, in the distance, a riddle appears,
A wave full of giggles, a chorus of cheers.
The crab's on a mission, in search of real bliss,
As the tide teases fate with a wink and a kiss.

So pack up your joy and sail to the far,
Where laughter is gold, and life's a bizarre.
On shores of illusion, the humor will rise,
And you'll find your heart dancing in endless skies.

## Longing for the Unreachable

I built a boat from a cereal box,
Set sail for dreams where the time never locks.
But the milk spilled over, oh what a sight,
Now I'm just drifting in my kitchen at night.

I waved to the clouds, they waved back with glee,
But they just laughed off my plan for a spree.
I tried to catch rainbows, but they slipped away,
Now I'm grounded, stuck until the next day.

## Lighthouses in the Mist

I sought a beacon amid the fluffy dew,
A lighthouse standing proud, guiding me too.
But the fog was thick with a comedy show,
As seagulls played peekaboo in the glow.

I followed a crab with a map made of sand,
Hoping it led to a treasure quite grand.
Instead, I found shells that whispered and pranced,
With jokes about humans not knowing to dance.

## Canvas of the Forgotten Sky

I splattered my dreams on a canvas so wide,
Colors of laughter, my funny pride.
The stars giggled softly, twinkling above,
While clouds carved out punchlines of innocent love.

The moon rolled its eyes at my brushstroke spree,
It said, "Dear Earthling, this isn't quite free!"
But I scribbled back tales of ages gone past,
Turning celestial bodies into a laugh fest.

## Starlit Canopies of Desire

Under starlit sheets that flutter and flip,
I dream of a journey, an intergalactic trip.
But my rocket is parked in the garage, you see,
Next to old bikes and a melted ice tea.

The galaxies twinkled with a wink and a nod,
While space mice danced with a half-eaten cod.
I laughed with a comet, we shared our best tales,
Yet here I remain, where the grass is for snails.

## Serenade of the Wandering Spirits

In a place where shadows play,
A ghost just lost its way.
He tripped over a broomstick,
And laughed until his bones went sick.

With a wink and a giggle,
He juggled some mist, oh so big!
The other ghosts rolled their eyes,
Saying, 'He can't even disguise!'

They danced on clouds like balloons,
Singing silly, outlandish tunes.
One tried to float up high,
But fell with a splat, oh my!

In the end, they climbed down quick,
Planning to give the moon a kick.
Yet in the night, they stayed up late,
Trading tales, sharing fate.

## Beyond the Canvas of the Sky.

Far up where the stars play chess,
A comet claimed it's the best,
But it sneezed and lost the game,
Now it's known for cosmic fame.

A cloud once decided to prance,
And spilled its rain in a dance.
Down below folks brought their hats,
Laughing with the jumping cats.

The sun grinned, a smile so wide,
While the moon waved, full of pride.
They traded jokes about the day,
Leaving the night in disarray.

And down below, the earth would sigh,
Accepting all the laughs up high.
In this land of giggles immense,
Every star shone with common sense.

## **Whispers of Distant Dreams**

The stars conspire, oh what fun,
Plotting mischief, one by one.
They tickle the dreams that float,
Making sleepy heads emote.

In the realm of snoozing knaves,
Lullabies turn into waves.
A bear in pajamas starts to dance,
Chasing fireflies, lost in a trance.

The moon wears a frown, quite wise,
Watching clumsy owls who rise.
They stumble on branches, oh dear me!
Who knew folks could climb a tree?

So when you dream of skies above,
Remember all that silly love.
For in the night, laughter streams,
With every whisper of your dreams.

## Echoes in the Twilight

In twilight's glow, the critters sing,
A frog called Don turned into a king.
He wore a crown made of a leaf,
Proclaiming, 'I'm the prince of beef!'

A cricket challenged him to a duel,
With a bow and arrow made of drool.
They laughed until the stars rolled out,
Joking 'What's this fuss about?'

The fireflies joined in with lights,
Throwing a party full of delights.
They served up moonlight and jelly beans,
Dancing around in wacky routines.

And when the day kissed night farewell,
The echoes lingered, cast a spell.
In that magical twilight scene,
Even ghosts found laughter keen.

## Bonds Across Distant Lands

In a land where llamas dance,
And socks are worn with no chance,
A postcard flies on a breeze,
Tickling toes of drowsy trees.

With penguins in a huddle tight,
They argue if it's day or night,
A kangaroo sipping tea,
Wonders if it's time to flee.

The snail is fast, or so he claims,
While playing odd and silly games,
Their laughter echoes, quite absurd,
A symphony of silly words.

At twilight's call, they sing a tune,
To cows who moonwalk under the moon,
In this land, love's a silly spree,
Where silly friends are all you need.

## Constellations in Solitude

Stars wear hats made out of cheese,
Winking down with cosmic tease,
An astronaut lost his shoe,
And that's why aliens hatched a coup.

On lazy nights with marshmallow dreams,
They plot and scheme in fluffy teams,
A comet trips on its own flame,
Turning space into a game.

Galaxies burst in giggles bright,
As planets join in goofy flight,
Planets dance and spin around,
Creating chaos, no sense found.

In solitude, they break the mold,
Stories of jest and joy retold,
With laughter echoing beyond the night,
The cosmos gleams with pure delight.

## Reveries of a Celestial Hearth

A hearth made of stardust gleams,
Where marshmallows float on moonbeams,
A dog in space wears silly hats,
While chatting softly with chubby rats.

In this realm, the owls wear ties,
As butterflies debate the skies,
They roast their acorns over flames,
And tell the best of silly names.

A comet plays the saxophone,
While rabbits tap dance all alone,
The galactic rhythms sway the night,
With laughter shared in pure delight.

Here dreams are whispered, and jokes unfold,
In cozy corners where stories are told,
A celestial hearth, bright and warm,
Where every giggle can transform.

## Whispers from the Other Side

Ghosts in capes sip lemonade,
While telling tales that never fade,
They sneak around with silly tricks,
Hiding behind the laughing bricks.

A troll is knitting on his bridge,
Claiming that he's now a smidge,
Fancy shoes for every dance,
With dancing snacks that share a glance.

Across the way, a gnome does flex,
While laughing at his broken specs,
With every whisper, tales take flight,
A world where nonsense feels just right.

To the other side, the secrets flow,
Where laughter's bright and time moves slow,
Whispers of mischief fill the air,
In this land, there's fun everywhere.

## Enchanted Eves of the Unreachable

On a hill where daydreams prance,
Cats wear hats and squirrels dance.
Magic spills from tea-tin pots,
Worms in bowties plotting lots.

Socks with stripes on every claw,
Juggling jellybeans, oh what a draw!
In a realm of giggles and cheer,
Naps are the currency here.

A fox with spectacles reads the news,
While owls debate on the best shoes.
All the toasts are made with cheese,
And laughter flows like a warm breeze.

So come and join this silly spree,
Where fish wear ties and dance with glee.
In each swirl of whimsy's delight,
We'll chase the clouds into the night.

## The Threshold of Wandering Souls


At the edge where spirits meet,
Chickens cluck in shoes that squeak.
Elders play hopscotch, quite a sight,
As candy rain falls day and night.

Gnomes sip tea, exchanging gabs,
While fairies trade both jests and jabs.
Echoes of laughter fill the air,
As the sun bounces without a care.

Balloons float by with silly faces,
Dancing round in wondrous paces.
Invisible friends, they join the game,
In this place, all feel the same.

When moonbeams twirl and shadows bend,
Even grumps find a joyful friend.
So waltz along the paths they roam,
Where wandering souls find their home.

## **Celestial Paths Untrodden**

Stars with smiles in the inky sky,
Comets whizzing, oh my, oh my!
Planets giggle in cosmic prance,
As asteroids waltz in a glittering dance.

Galaxies swirl in colorful song,
While meteors hum, "We all belong."
A turtle in sunglasses takes the lead,
Saying, "Slow down, let's plant a seed!"

In this realm of stardust delight,
Even comets sip tea every night.
Cakes made of moons and cosmic pies,
Tickle your taste with sugar highs.

So soar through this whimsical spree,
Where dreams are wild and spirits free.
In the dance of the stars, we twirl,
In a universe of joy, we whirl.

## Hues of Dusk and Dawn

When day dips low and night takes flight,
Crickets wear shades, quite a sight.
Fireflies flash like disco lights,
Chasing laughter into starry nights.

At dawn, toast pops with a cheer,
Butterflies giggle, "Breakfast is here!"
Coffee brews with a dance and a wail,
Cats in pajamas, they tell a tale.

Morning news is all a game,
With biscuits and jam worth all the fame.
Time ticks away on rubber bands,
As we frolic in no-man's lands.

So catch the laughter in the air,
Where colors mingle without a care.
In dusk's embrace, the day doth yawn,
Let the hues play till the break of dawn.

## Where Horizons Converge

A place where skies meet the ground,
Socks worn differently, laughter's sound.
Cats on rooftops planning a heist,
Chasing shadows, rolling in rice.

We built a bridge with silly strings,
Eagles compete with rubber flings.
A picnic spread with jam and cheese,
With ants drafting laws to appease.

Dancing squirrels in tuxedo suits,
Debating cheese puffs versus roots.
Neighborhood watch with binoculars,
Finding gnomes and suspicious cars.

At dusk, the sea plays peek-a-boo,
While turtles play cards with chilly stew.
The moon winks at our silly games,
As we giggle through the sparkly flames.

## Footsteps on the Edge of Dawn

Morning whispers in colors bright,
Coffee spills in a clumsy fight.
We tiptoe on beams of golden light,
Chasing roosters that take flight.

A dog in pajamas joins the race,
Chasing his tail with curious grace.
Then comes a frog in a tiny hat,
Singing louder than a bratty cat.

Counting the clouds as they drift by,
One looks like popcorn, one like pie.
The sun blushes as we yell 'Surprise!'
With confetti tossed at sleepy skies.

Who knew dawn could be this much fun?
Kites made of pizza, oh what a run!
We dance and twirl, heedless of the morn,
As the day giggles, newly born.

## Conversations with the Infinite

I said hello to a cosmic duck,
It quacked back, 'You're out of luck!'
The stars giggled, playing hide and seek,
While planets hummed a funky beat.

Black holes joked they'd steal our lunch,
Consumed by gravity, oh what a punch!
The galaxy swirled with tales of yore,
Teachers teaching space and more.

As I sipped my starlit tea,
A comet asked, 'Would you like to flee?'
Off to the land of hiccuping moons,
Where mermaids danced to cartoon tunes.

The universe smiled, a knowing grin,
Whispered secrets hidden within.
Time traveled by in socks with stripes,
As laughter echoed through cosmic pipes.

## **Beyond the Veil of Extrasensory**

In a realm where colors taste like sighs,
Whispers float and surf like flies.
I tried to pet a giggling breeze,
It tickled my nose, danced through the trees.

The wind told tales of donut spills,
While shadows played with funny quills.
Invisible cats chased sunny rays,
While I wondered about my misplaced trays.

Mirrors laugh at their own reflections,
Creating baffling, wild connections.
I asked a cloud where dreams reside,
It replied with a flip and a slide.

Time wears a hat that's two sizes too big,
While clocks learn to dance like a jolly gig.
In this space, logic took a break,
As I baked cookies with a friendly cake.

## Navigating Through the Clouds

In a boat made of dreams, we sail so high,
Chasing cotton candy and marshmallow sky.
The compass is broken, but that's quite okay,
We'll just follow the giggles, come what may.

A map drawn in crayons, with paths full of fun,
We'll race with the rainbows, we'll never outrun.
Jump over the puddles, leap spirits afloat,
On the wings of our laughter, we happily gloat.

With clouds as our pillows, we nap in the blue,
Snoring the symphonies of giggles anew.
But watch out for starlings, they might try to steal,
The snacks in our pockets, our lunchtime meal.

So here we float lightly, with our silly crew,
In this buoyant parade, there's room for a few.
We'll dance with the breezes, spin laughter galore,
In the boat made of dreams, we just want some more.

## Pages Turning in the Ether

In a library floating on giggles and glee,
The pages are whispering secrets to me.
Each flap of a cover makes a whooping sound,
As the words jump around, they're perfectly round.

A feathered quill quivers, it wiggles with pause,
As I pen in the margins what life really was.
The ink starts to laugh, it splatters and twirls,
Painting portraits of mischief, in wild, wavy swirls.

A bookmark of socks lies between tales of traction,
Tripping through stories in all different factions.
With each twist and turn, a chuckle comes free,
As the plot thickens nicely like warm, creamy tea.

So let's grab a volume, let's read with delight,
In ether we'll frolic, 'till day turns to night.
With laughter as our guide, we'll dive deep and explore,
As pages keep turning, we'll always want more.

## Mirage of the Wandering Heart

Once I saw a mirage, oh what a fine sight,
It winked and it skedaddled, just out of my light.
With a heart made of jelly, I chased it around,
In a garden where giggles and dreams can be found.

It danced on the daisies, spun in the breeze,
Said, 'Catch me, oh please!' with such comical ease.
But my feet made of pudding just wobbled and flopped,
And laughter erupted, I stumbled, I dropped.

With a grin, it took off, a giggly escape,
As I chased through the flowers, in comical shape.
We played hide and seek, with winks and with grins,
In the mirage of dreams, where adventure begins.

If ever you wander and hear laughter near,
Know that a mirage is always quite clear.
It tickles the heart and makes giggles take flight,
In the land of the whimsical, everything's right.

## The Last Stop Before the Stars

On a bus made of bubbles, we travel with glee,
With seats full of marshmallows, just you and me.
We'll ride past the planets, and zoom past the moons,
While singing our favorite, most silly of tunes.

The driver's a cat wearing glasses and ties,
He winks as he drives and gives kittens the skies.
With a swish and a swash, he takes us for a spin,
As laughter erupts from all the joy within.

We stop for a moment at Gigglewood Lane,
Where the trees drop confetti and sprout candy cane.
With ice cream for tickets, we clap and we cheer,
As we bounce on the clouds, no worries, no fear.

So if you are ready for a ride full of cheer,
Join us on this bus, let's take you near.
To the last stop of wonders where dreams meet the stars,
In this world of pure joy, we've got all the jars!

## **Traces of a Fading Path**

There once was a road, all covered in dust,
Where cars found their rest, in a chariot rust.
With signs that were bent, but still stood so grand,
They pointed to places no one could quite stand.

Old ladies would giggle, as they passed it by,
Saying, "This road leads to the pie in the sky!"
With every pothole, a mystery brewed,
Like a game of charades, misspoken and rude.

Yet there were some travelers, brave and quite bold,
Who sought out the stories that legends foretold.
But where they had gone, was just a big joke,
As they wandered and laughed, over trails they chose to poke.

So if you should wander, through fields full of glee,
Remember that path, that doesn't quite agree.
For sometimes the journey breaks laughter in twain,
And a fading old road brings the best kind of pain.

## Symphony of the Endless Space

In a world where the stars would dance in a line,
A jester was born, named Fred of the Vine.
He tickled the moons and he strummed on a star,
While planets did jiggles as goofy as bizarre.

Saturn's rings jingled with each little beat,
While comets spun around in circles so sweet.
The sun would just wink, trying not to intrude,
On Fred's cosmic jam, like a fun-loving dude.

Yet, as Fred played louder, the black holes would grumble,
"Hey, keep it down, Fred! Or we're all going to tumble!"
But Fred just laughed on, with a wink and a spin,
For in endless vastness, there's room for the grin.

So next time you gaze at the twinkling night,
Remember the jester, who brought lots of light.
In symphonies echoing through galaxies wide,
There's humor and joy, on this cosmic ride!

# Keys to the Boundless Horizon

A locksmith named Joe had some keys made of cheese,
He'd giggle and titter as he tossed them with ease.
In pockets he carried, a mix of dessert,
Unlocking the laughter, with smiles and some hurt.

He'd offer a key to the clouds passing by,
"Oh open up, friends! Let's all give it a try!"
But the clouds just chuckled and floated away,
Leaving Joe and his keys to continue their play.

He'd try to unlock all the dreams in the sky,
With keys that were melting, making pigeons cry.
"Who knew cheese-disguised could bring laughter so grand?"
As rain turned to cheddar, across all the land.

So if you should meet him, remember his scheme,
A key made of cheese can unlock every dream.
For laughter, dear friends, is the brightest of keys,
In a world full of whimsy like melting cheese breeze.

## The Mark of Celestial Footprints

There lived a strange fella named Gus from the moon,
With one giant foot, he'd stomp, tap, and croon.
He'd walk on the stars without making a sound,
Leaving laughter and giggles in circles around.

Each step that he took sent asteroids twirling,
And comets, they winked, like a big disco swirling.
With footprints of glitter, he left quite a trail,
A cosmic connection, where humor won't fail.

Yet some thought it odd, a giant's parade,
As planets would chuckle and aliens played.
"Watch where you're treading!" they'd holler and cheer,
As stardust was scattered from Gus's big rear.

But Gus just kept dancing, with joy as his muse,
Over mountains of starlight and jungles of blues.
So if you spot footprints up there in the night,
Remember old Gus, and his silly delight!

## Serenity in the Twilight Glow

In twilight's light, the ducks debate,
Whether to swim or to simply wait.
A frog on a lily, with dreams of flight,
Sings to the moon, it's quite the sight.

The fireflies giggle in a dance so bright,
As crickets hold concerts till the night.
A pickle jar floats with plans so grand,
To sail the breeze—just as it had planned.

Meanwhile, a hedgehog spins tales so tall,
About wandering stars and a cosmic ball.
He claims he met aliens with hats made of cheese,
But most just believe he's lost in the breeze.

As day turns to night, the silliness peaks,
With shadows that waltz and darkness that squeaks.
Under the giggles of old, wise trees,
Serenity reigns, carried by the breeze.

## **Thresholds to Imagined Retreats**

At the edge of dreams, a slide made of light,
Leads to a kingdom of giggles and fright.
Where socks hold debates on the best color scheme,
And pillows engage in a competitive dream.

A cat wearing glasses reads books upside down,
While turtles race at a leisurely brown.
Here the wildflowers don hats made of cake,
And dance in a line, raising quite the quake.

The moon serves pancakes, the sun brews some tea,
As clouds play hopscotch, giggling in glee.
Tickle the stars, give the night a good poke,
In a world where laughter is the magic folk's cloak.

So pack up your quirks and take a leap wide,
Into this retreat where the sillies abide.
With joy as the compass and smiles as the map,
You'll find there's no end to the fun and the sap.

## The Enclave of Faded Memories

In an attic of giggles, where dust bunnies roam,
Old toys hold a court, claiming this is their home.
A bear with a monocle grumbles with glee,
Recalling the times he was a child's decree.

The marbles engage in a rolling debate,
While old shoes reminisce, reliving their fate.
A clock chimes out jokes from the old days of yore,
Tickling the rafters, who laugh and implore.

In the corner, a photo of smiles long past,
Waves at the future, bringing giggles to cast.
With umbrellas that whisper and slippers that dance,
This enclave of laughter invites you to prance.

So when the shadows stretch and the laughter grows loud,

Join the whispers of memory, they're seldom too proud.
In the heart of the old, you'll find joy still thrives,
With echoes of fun, where silliness thrives.

## Breath of Ancients Beyond

In a realm of breezes where giggles are old,
Ancient trees whisper tales, quite bold.
A squirrel with wisdom, donning a crown,
Shares secrets of nuts from the days of renown.

Mushrooms make muffins and serve up delight,
While shadows play peek-a-boo, twisting in light.
With each secret giggle, a leaf takes a leap,
And joins the ballet, with rhythms to keep.

Old rocks crack worn jokes, with laughter so deep,
While rivers sing songs that wake the steep.
They spin yarns of the winds that tickle the lake,
And watch as the clouds form a crew for a break.

So wander the realms of these sillies up high,
Where laughter is ancient, and jokes never die.
From the whispers of flora to fauna's hum,
Join in the jest where the fun's never numb.

## Gardens in the Distance

In fields where sunflowers start to chat,
A rabbit offers wisdom, wearing a hat.
The carrots debate on who's the best,
While squirrels proclaim they need a rest.

A hedgehog plays chess with a passing breeze,
While roses gossip about squirrels' keys.
Laughter erupts from daisies so bright,
As they plan a dance under the moonlight.

The daisies joke, 'Let's serve some tea!'
While butterflies flap like they're on a spree.
A worm dreams of becoming a star,
Yet here he is, still stuck in the jar.

From beyond the trees, a wind chimes in,
With stories of chickens wearing a grin.
With laughter that echoes, the day drifts away,
In gardens where nonsense leads the play.

## Luminescence of Nevermore

At dusk, the owls play hide and seek,
A fish gives an impressionist critique.
Moonbeams drape a cloak on a snail,
As it prints stars on a forgotten trail.

The shadows argue who's the most sly,
While glowbugs dance, and the crickets sigh.
A total eclipse of the moon starts to wink,
As frogs tell secrets over coffee and ink.

Nocturnal cats hold a talcum powder fight,
While wise squirrels deem it a sight, sheer delight.
A coyote reveals his dreams of fame,
But here he is, still chasing the same.

Under this cloak where the laughter tones,
Odd creatures engage in philosophical phones.
The night unravels with jokes and guffaws,
In a luminescence that breaks all the laws.

## Fables from the Edge of Existence

A turtle recites verses, slow and clear,
While moles ponder existential fear.
A kite made of dreams sails high with a giggle,
As ants shuffle by, doing a dance-like wiggle.

A mischievous fox holds a tale of woe,
About a squirrel who danced on a toe.
The moon snickers at stories both wise and absurd,
In a world where the laughter is largely unheard.

A wise old owl claims to know it all,
Yet drops his glasses—oh, what a fall!
The tales come alive as feelings ignite,
In a comforting chaos, where wrongs can be right.

Each fable spins wild, with twists galore,
Leave your logic behind; who could ask for more?
A squirrel in a suit insists on the dance,
While the absurdity claims us as its chance.

## Whirlwinds of Untamed Roads

In whirlwinds, the tumbleweeds hold a race,
With cactus wearin' a grin on its face.
A barbecue's lit by a confused raccoon,
While ants debate the worth of a moon.

The pathways twist like a silly old joke,
Where boulders contemplate if they're just a hoax.
Grasshoppers throw confetti with glee,
While singing about things that they hope to see.

An owl on a moped revs up with flair,
As llamas weave tales from the folding chair.
Chasing horizons where the sun likes to play,
In a whirlwind dance that brightens the day.

Every bump tells a story, each turn a plot,
With laughs echoing through the untamed lot.
In a realm where oddities reign supreme,
A road of whims leads to a chuckling dream.

## Echoes in the Air

In a land where socks have pairs,
And cows play cards in foolish glares,
I lost my keys beneath a chair,
The echoes laugh, as if they care.

A cat with boots can dance a jig,
While puppies debate the size of swigs,
A frog tells tales of dancing pigs,
And time stands still, like an old twig.

The clouds wear hats and tap their feet,
While rainbows run a groovy beat,
A snail insists it's quick, not fleet,
And life's a joke, both sly and sweet.

So let us linger, laugh, and play,
In this strange world where nonsense sways,
We'll laugh at all the silly ways,
And cherish joy in bright arrays.

## Crossroads of Dreams and Destiny

At the rev'd-up junction of the mind,
Where dreams are lost and then redefined,
A chicken crossed, got quite entwined,
Now clucks out plans, oh so maligned.

The squirrels plot with acorn schemes,
While daisies giggle in sunlight beams,
A hedgehog spins his grandball dreams,
While clouds float past in goofy teams.

Pick a path, do the jig or twist,
But guard your snacks, as they persist,
For mischief's great, you can't resist,
At this wild crossroad, you'll be missed.

Follow the signs that dance and tease,
With wobbly steps, do as you please,
For laughter's wind is blowing free,
In this bonkers maze of destiny.

## Sojourn at Day's Outskirts

Out by the edge of mishaps galore,
Where ducks wear ties and eagles soar,
I found a frog who sells décor,
And giggles spring from every door.

The sun throws pies, in silly cheer,
While owls debate if they're sincere,
A garden gnome is dancing near,
As time, it ticks, but none adhere.

A picnic blanket talks of dreams,
As ants declare their sugar schemes,
While clouds dissect their fluffy seams,
And life feels good with all its beams.

So come, let's wander, hop, and sway,
In this odd realm where we can play,
With smiles wide and worries gray,
Let's frolic in a goofy way.

## **Fantasies Tethered to Reality**

In a world where jellybeans rain,
Tales of flying pies seem quite insane,
A fish on stripes declares a train,
While frogs in hats all sing the same.

The moon spins tales of mighty knights,
While cats dish gossip on moonlight nights,
A dog insists he's right in fights,
And laughter echoes, oh what sights!

With dreams that bounce and whirl like kites,
Reality wears mismatched tights,
Where elephants debate their heights,
And all of life feels full of delights.

So tethered here, let's toast our cheer,
Embrace the fun, the wacky sphere,
For in this realm, no hint of fear,
Just giggles shared as friends draw near.

## Secrets of the Faraway Nest

In a tree that leans and sways,
A squirrel speaks in funny ways.
He's hiding acorns, what a chap!
With stories tucked in his little cap.

The birds debate over who can sing,
While ants march by with things to bring.
The whispers travel through the breeze,
As owls chuckle from the trees.

A rabbit hops, and oh, what flair!
He tells tall tales without a care.
The grass tickles his bunny feet,
As he shares jokes, oh what a treat!

So if you wander, keep your ears,
For gags and giggles fill the years.
In that nest, a world so bright,
Full of laughter, pure delight.

## Shadows at Daybreak

At dawn's light, the shadows play,
They twist and jump in a funny way.
A cat's leap sends them running fast,
As the sun peeks in, the night is past.

A dog snorts loud, trying to chase,
His own tail in a frantic race.
The shadows giggle, dart, and dance,
While the world wakes up, given the chance.

A gopher pops up, what a surprise,
With puzzled looks in his small eyes.
He trips on shadows, falls in a heap,
And dreams of sleep—oh, not so deep!

But flickering light begins to win,
As shadows fade, they laugh and grin.
What a show that morning brings,
Chasing light with silly things!

## Gaze Upon the Unseen

If you look past the bushes and weeds,
You'll find a place where laughter breeds.
With creatures plotting silly schemes,
And dancing flowers, bursting seams.

A hedgehog juggles tiny stones,
While frogs debate their funny tones.
The rabbits wear their finest hats,
And gossip like the silliest rats.

A creature whispers, 'What's that smell?'
It's just the flowers, who laugh so well.
They twist and shout in vibrant bloom,
Creating giggles in every room.

So wander near where shadows gleam,
And witness all, or just a dream.
For if you peek beyond the green,
You'll find the joy of the unseen.

## Reflections of a Forgotten Realm

In a pond where the ripples tease,
Frogs sit back, sipping their teas.
They dressed in suits, quite dapper and neat,
Discussing politics over a beet.

The fishes swim with no care in sight,
While dragonflies buzz, oh what a fright!
They dance around with glittering glee,
Like tiny pilots, soaring free.

Mice bring cheese for the grand buffet,
While all join in for a silly play.
The sun sets low, creating a scene,
Of laughter echoing—the great routine.

So if you find a hidden glade,
Where these odd friends are never swayed,
Join in the fun, don't be too far,
And laugh aloud, like a shining star.

## The Gateway of Silent Stories

In a realm where whispers play,
The tales are waltzing, come what may.
A cat in boots with a hat so high,
Chasing shadows that giggle and fly.

Chairs are gossiping, what a sight!
As spoons conspire to take their flight.
The carpet dances, oh what a tease,
While the curtains laugh at all with ease.

Here the clock ticks in silly rhymes,
With every hour, it changes times.
The walls are painted with laughter's hue,
While paintings wink just to joke with you.

So step right in, join this odd fest,
Where stories linger, never to rest.
In this place, time twirls like a kite,
And every whisper tickles with delight.

## **Beneath the Stretching Skies**

Beneath the skies that stretch and sway,
Clouds make shapes that dance and play.
A rhino struts with a top hat grand,
Claiming, 'I'm ruler of this vast land!'

The sun is grinning, holding a cup,
Sipping sunshine, then lighting up.
Rainbows gossip, dressing the air,
While trees wear socks, a quirky pair.

Birds are tweeting their own sweet tunes,
Joking about the man in the moon.
A squirrel cracks jokes from the high branches,
While ants take turns in their odd dances.

Every breeze carries laughter's sound,
With a sprinkle of joy that knows no bound.
In this whimsical charade, take a seat,
Where every heartbeat feels like a treat.

## Porches of Untold Journeys

On porches wide with creaky chairs,
Lies a traveler who spins wild flares.
He claims to have seen a dancing cloud,
And a cactus that danced in a crowd.

His stories tickle the evening air,
Of llamas wearing pajamas in pairs.
He sips lemonade with a wink and grin,
While beetles meet for a violin spin.

The fireflies gather for a pop-up show,
In the glow of the porch, they put on a glow.
Expecting applause, they flicker their lights,
Hoping for cheers during warm summer nights.

So lean back tight in this boundless space,
Where tales are shared with a whimsical grace.
Every moment here feels like a flight,
To lands of laughter, oh what a sight!

## Windows to Tomorrow's Light

Through windows wide, oh what do we find?
Nonsense and giggles, all well-defined.
Monkeys are juggling with grapes on a line,
While mice offer cheese with a twist of lime.

A rainbow squirrel runs for the bake,
Romancing the muffins, oh for goodness' sake!
Cookies wink as they dance on the tray,
In this merriment game, they all want to play.

Outside the pane, bubbles float and twirl,
With a frog in a suit giving it a whirl.
He croaks out rhymes, oh so absurd,
Chasing after the tales he's heard.

So peek through these frames of delight and cheer,
Each glance reveals a new frontier.
In a land where laughter reaches new heights,
Tomorrow's light is all about sights!

## The Haven Where the Sky Meets Earth

In a land where clouds take naps,
And rainbows hang like curtain drapes,
The sun wears shades and struts around,
While giggling skies throw silly shapes.

Kites dance like cats on a sugar high,
While hills roll over, chasing bees,
A place where laughter's always loud,
And trees gossip with dancing leaves.

Even the stones crack jokes on walks,
As streams murmur tales of mischief,
It's where the stars wear glitter hats,
And shadows craft their own comic strips.

So pack your dreams in a backpack,
And bring your slippers made of clouds,
We'll sip moonlit kaleidoscope tea,
In this haven, laughter's always proud.

## Sheltering Stars in the Night

When twilight settles on the ground,
The stars come out for a midnight snack,
They sit on rooftops, sharing pies,
And joke with owls in their twilight pack.

Bats play tag with the shivering moon,
While squirrels sing their bedtime tunes,
The planets spin in disco tricks,
And dreams get tangled like mischievous looms.

Nearby, fireflies hold a dance,
With twinkling lights and daring glances,
The night wears a goofy grin,
As shadows break into silly prances.

Every corner whispers secrets sweet,
Under the glow of erratic stars,
In this shelter of cosmic wit,
Pure joy is measured by our avatars.

## Homes of Wandering Dreams

In a realm where wishes float like boats,
Dreams skip stones on crystal streams,
With pillows made from clouds of hope,
They bounce around like playful beams.

The walls are filled with painted laughs,
As giggling suns tan sleepy moons,
Each corner hosts a wild parade,
While time spins yarns with its cartoons.

Puppies dangle from chandeliers,
And candy canes sprout from the ground,
Wandering fancies slide around,
Manifesting goofiness all around.

So build your dreams with silly schemes,
And hold them tight, don't let them slip,
In homes of wonder, laughter beams,
Join the fiesta—let life rip!

## Beyond the Veil of Dusk

As the day hides behind the smirk,
The worlds collide in playful jest,
With shadows boasting silly tricks,
And the wind wears a sunflower vest.

Here, giggles echo through the trees,
While whispers dance on fairy wings,
The dusk god juggle with stars anew,
As night's chorus sweetly sings.

Clouds shoot confetti in the breeze,
And breezes blow a friendly tune,
In this quirky twilight wonder,
Every moment's a fun festoon.

So if you seek a laugh or two,
Come wander past the day's decline,
The veil of dusk invites you here,
To joy that sparkles like fine wine.

## Between the Gates of Uncertainty

A garden gnome with a silly grin,
Decides it's time for a little spin.
He waltzes through flowers, ignores the bees,
While squirrels laugh hard, hanging from trees.

The mailbox sings tunes of outdated news,
While lawn flamingos debate their shoes.
They gossip and chatter 'bout neighborly woes,
And trade stories of the last hedge clippings' grows.

A cat in sunglasses claims he's the king,
While chasing his tail, what a funny thing!
Beneath the fence lies a rabbit with flair,
Dressed in a tux, he just doesn't care.

A dog barks loud from a porch made of wood,
Swears he is guarding the best neighborhood.
But in the bushes, the raccoons cheer,
Plotting a heist for the pizza I fear.

## Visions at the Edge of Night

Under the moon, the owls throw a rave,
While shadows do dances, it's quite the wave.
The stars come down, looking quite uncouth,
With sparkly outfits that yield no truth.

A bat in a top hat says, "Join the cause!"
While a hedgehog juggles—the crowd just claws.
The popcorn pops loud like it's true art,
As fireflies twinkle with a flickering heart.

The wind starts to giggle, a mischievous breeze,
As clouds play peek-a-boo, oh what a tease!
At dawn's early light, the laughter will cease,
But until then, let's dance with no lease.

"Who let the dogs out?" the coyotes declare,
They bask in their fame like they haven't a care.
As night turns to day, they strut to their beat,
In visions of fun that they can't be beat.

## A Shelter of Celestial Light

A UFO's here, throwing a cookout,
With Martians and humans sharing a sprout.
They roast marshmallows with cosmic delight,
While giggling comets shoot across the night.

A pancake planet flips high in the sky,
As jellyfish float by, oh my oh my!
The moon hops along with a bounce and a twist,
While giggling stars say, "You can't be missed!"

A racquetball match with a satellite,
As aliens cheer, they've got the right light.
They serve with a laugh in an intergalactic dome,
While robots bring snacks from their faraway home.

The sun peeks in, with a whimsical grin,
"Did I miss anything?" it cheekily spins.
With laughter so bright, it's a celestial sight,
Where fun fills the air as day fades to night.

## Rooms of Forgotten Reveries

In a room full of socks, mismatched and bold,
They gather for stories that never get old.
The slippers chime in, debating their fate,
While dust bunnies plan a grand dinner date.

A chair reclines low with a creaky old sigh,
"Did you hear the news? Our fridge can fly!"
The curtains all gossip about yesterday's sun,
And how it won't party—now that's just no fun.

The walls are adorned with pictures of cats,
Who clutch at their whiskers, they're all aristocrats.
Each painting's a tale of how grand they once dreamt,
With laughter echoing, a perfect precept.

In corners of memory, the dust motes play tag,
With shadows and whispers, all under a rag.
In this quirky abode, the laughter's a gem,
Where nobody's serious and fun's at the helm.

www.ingramcontent.com/pod-product-compliance
Lightning Source LLC
Chambersburg PA
CBHW070312120526
44590CB00017B/2650